Superstars!
Superstars!
Superstars!
Superstars!

CREATIVE EDUCATION SPORTS SUPERSTARS

roger
staubach
roger
staubach
roger
staubach

roger staubach

by Jay H. Smith
illustrated by
Harold Henriksen

CREATIVE EDUCATION
MANKATO, MINNESOTA

Published by Creative Education, 123 South Broad Street, P. O. Box 227,
Mankato, Minnesota 56001

Copyright © 1974 by Creative Education. International copyrights reserved in all countries.
No part of this book may be reproduced in any form without written permission
from the publisher. Printed in the United States.
Distributed by Childrens Press, 1224 West Van Buren Street, Chicago, Illinois 60607
Library of Congress Number: 74-13134   ISBN: 0-87191-378-X

Cover: Photo by Vernon J. Biever

Library of Congress Cataloging in Publication Data
Smith, Jay H   Roger Staubach.
SUMMARY: Traces Roger Staubach's rise to number one quarterback of the
Dallas Cowboys after joining the team as a twenty-seven-year-old rookie
following four years in Vietnam.
1. Staubach, Roger, 1942- —Juvenile literature.   2. Football—Juvenile literature
[1. Staubach, Roger, 1942-   2. Football—Biography]
I. Henriksen, Harold, illus. II. Title.
GV939.S733S63   796.33'2'0924 [B] [92]   74-13134
ISBN 0-87191-378-X

On a typical workday in 1968, clerks at the office of the Dallas Cowboys busily sorted through what seemed to be a mountain of mail. Among the letters so full of requests that simply could not be granted, was one from a Navy officer stationed in Vietnam. He wanted the Cowboys to send him a "Duke" football, the official National Football League (NFL) model.

This was one request the Dallas Cowboys were happy to grant, for the writer of the letter was none other than Roger Staubach.

The Cowboys wasted no time in sending the football to Staubach, who was serving as the officer in charge of a supply depot near Da Nang. There, during off-duty hours, the man who one day would lead Dallas to victory in the Super Bowl practiced his passing on the dusty roads of war-torn Vietnam.

Vietnam was far away in time and space from the scene of Roger Staubach's days of football glory. As an All-American quarterback at the Naval Academy in the early 1960's, he had distinguished himself as the most exciting college football player of his time.

Staubach was now finishing his third year of active duty with the Navy. In another year his mandatory 4-year tour would be over.

Then he would have to make the important decision he had thought so seriously about since graduating from the Academy. Would he re-enlist in the Navy and make it his career, or would he gamble on his future and try to play pro football?

It was a difficult decision for Staubach to make. He loved the Navy. To leave it would mean giving up a great deal he had worked and studied so hard to attain.

But football was in his blood, and he had to find out if he could make it as a pro. A year later, when a reporter asked him what had prompted his decision, Roger said, "If I hadn't tried to play pro ball, I would have spent my whole life wondering if I could have."

Although Roger's faith in his ability never wavered, he recognized that there were several obstacles in his path to the NFL. First of all, he would be 27 by the time he was ready to play for Dallas. This was rather late to be a raw rookie trying to learn the sophisticated pro game.

He knew, too, that no one had ever come back to make it in the pros after such a long absence from competitive football. After all, Roger had played his last game at the Naval Academy in the fall of 1964.

Although he had trained faithfully throughout his career in the Navy, Roger had to admit he was rusty. Daily workouts of running and lifting weights had helped, of course.

He had thrown 400 passes a day anywhere he found a willing receiver — whether on the slippery deck of a ship or on the smooth turf of a parade ground. This helped him maintain his passing accuracy. But Roger had missed the one thing that would have kept him at his peak — the pressure of actual game experience.

Roger had to acknowledge still a third difficulty — the Cowboys were rich in top-flight quarterbacks. Don Meredith, the team's starter, had established himself as one of the league's best. Back-up quarterback, Craig Morton,

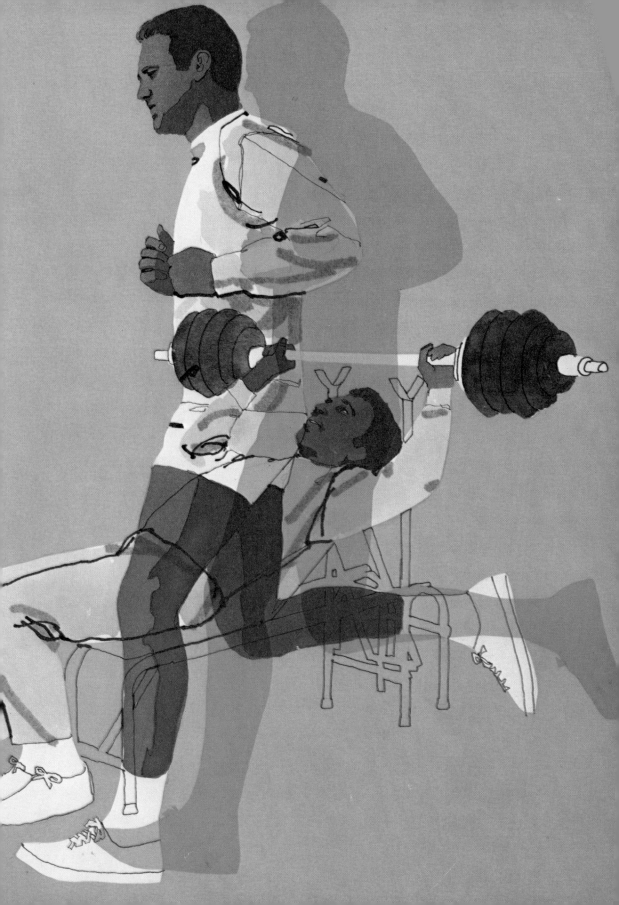

was a fine passer with 4 years of NFL experience. Even Jerry Rhome, the third-string quarterback, had to be rated ahead of Staubach at this point.

Roger's prospects of even making the Dallas team looked slim indeed, but he wasn't discouraged. Looking forward to the pressure and competition ahead of him, Roger notified the Cowboys that he would be ready to play when training camp opened in July, 1969.

Shortly before training camp began, Dallas announced the trade of Jerry Rhome to another NFL team. This move automatically elevated Staubach to the Number 3 position among the team's quarterbacks. But more important than that, it indicated to Roger that Head Coach Tom Landry had confidence in him. Roger felt sure he would be worthy of that confidence.

When they heard that Staubach would be joining the team, football fans in Dallas were overjoyed. Although it had been 4 long years since the gifted quarterback had dominated the headlines, his name was still magic.

Many fans recalled Roger's sterling performance against the University of Texas Longhorns in the Cotton Bowl game on January 1, 1964. Even though his Naval Academy squad had lost the game, Roger's individual exploits had won the hearts of the partisan Texas crowd. His

21 pass completions for 228 yards had set a new Cotton Bowl Record.

It wasn't only Roger's thrilling passing and daring scrambling that made him so uniquely popular. Dallas fans admired his coolness under pressure. They could identify with this crew-cut, genuinely humble, deeply religious young man. He was their idea of what a player should be.

It didn't take long before letters began to pour into the Dallas Cowboy office, advising Coach Landry to give Roger every opportunity to make the team. Staubach had a well-deserved reputation as winner, and these fans felt this was exactly what the Cowboys needed.

Loyal Dallas fans were frustrated. For 3 straight seasons the talented Cowboys had come close, but every year they had let the coveted championship slip away. In both 1966 and 1967, Dallas had gone all the way to the NFL championship game, only to be defeated by the mighty Green Bay Packers.

In 1968 the Cowboys had won their third consecutive division title, only to be subdued by Cleveland in the Eastern championship game.

Cowboy fans were clamoring for a change. They believed that the star-studded team was potentially the best in the league. All Dallas needed, they said, was a truly

outstanding leader. To some of the fans, Staubach was just the man to transform the team into the very best in all of football.

Tom Landry — an unemotional, reasonable man — did not entirely disagree with that evaluation of Staubach. Yes, of course, he would give Roger every chance to earn a place on the team.

But Landry was certain that Roger, like any other rookie, had a great deal to learn about the pro system. All of that would take time; and the patient, methodical Landry was determined to bring Roger along slowly and carefully.

While it normally takes 5 years for a player to develop into a complete pro quarterback, Landry predicted that the mature Staubach would do it in 3. "It will take

him that long to read defenses clearly," the Dallas coach said.

With the opening of the Dallas training camp, Roger Staubach took his first steps on the road to NFL stardom.

Every day after practice had officially ended, Roger stayed on the field, throwing passes until the very last receiver had quit for the day. He never seemed to tire. There wasn't time to think about physical strain. Motivated solely by the desire to make up for lost time, Roger worked harder than he ever had before.

The rookie quarterback quickly won the respect of the veteran Cowboy players. What impressed them most was his incredible determination to succeed.

Although Roger's return to football was one of the happiest times in his life, it was not without many painful moments of frustration and sadness.

He was almost always alone in training camp. Because he was older and more mature, Roger found it hard to make friends with his fellow rookies. He had little in common with them. They were carefree bachelors; he was a married man with 3 young children. They had just left college; he had recently returned from the war.

Because he was a rookie who still had to prove himself, Roger found a great deal of personal distance between the veteran players and himself. Adding to the problem was Roger's serious and withdrawn nature.

Training had been underway for only a few weeks when Don Meredith announced his retirement from football. Everyone associated with the team was stunned by the news.

At 31, Meredith was at the age when NFL quarterbacks usually reach their peak. Moreover, 1968 had been the best season of his 9-year career. His decision to quit seemed incomprehensible.

But Meredith, one of the league's most frequently injured players, had simply had enough. Football was no longer fun, and he just didn't want another season in the bruising NFL.

With Meredith's departure, an intense rivalry sprang up between Staubach and Craig Morton. Fortunately the rivalry was purely professional. The 2 men got along fairly well together, even though Roger always felt somewhat uncomfortable about their relationship. "It's hard to be friends with someone whose job I'm trying to take away," he said.

Both Morton and Staubach had finished their college careers in 1964. They had played against each other in several All-Star games with Roger usually getting most of the fanfare.

In those days he had over-shadowed every college quarterback in the country including Morton. When only a junior, Roger had won the Heisman Trophy, an award honoring the outstanding college player of the year.

Things were entirely different now. The roles were reversed, and Craig Morton was in control.

Behind the passing of Morton, the Cowboys raced undefeated through the first 4 games of the 1969 exhibition schedule. Staubach spent most of his time observing from the Dallas bench.

Late in the second quarter of the fifth preseason contest, Morton was hit hard by the charging New York Jet defense. The blow dislocated the index finger of his passing hand.

With a little over a minute to play in the half, Staubach was sent into the game. Moving as adeptly as a veteran, Roger took the Cowboys 76 yards for the score. It was a dramatic debut for the rookie.

The final exhibition game proved an embarrassing experience for Roger. The alert Baltimore Colt zone defense fooled him repeatedly, intercepting 4 of his passes.

There was one bright spot, however. Roger did get a chance to demonstrate his great speed and mobility, amassing over 100 yards rushing. But that gave him little solace; for when the game had ended, the Colts walked off the field with a 23-7 victory.

After the game Roger said, "I think I learned more tonight than I've learned in all my years in football."

Since Morton was still unable to play, Roger had a chance to redeem himself in the regular season opener against the St. Louis Cardinals. Regaining the poise that had deserted him in the Colt game, Roger led the Cowboys to a convincing 24-3 win. One Dallas touchdown had come on a 75-yard Staubach bomb to speedy Lance Rentzel.

But Roger's days as the starting quarterback were numbered. Morton's injury had healed, and the veteran quarterback was ready for Dallas' second game with the New Orleans Saints.

For the remainder of the season Morton was in command. Starting every game, he led Dallas to its fourth straight division title. Individually, Morton finished the regular season ranking fifth among NFL passers.

What had been a fine year turned sour in the Eastern Conference championship game. The Cowboys' play-off jinx prevailed; and they were slaughtered by the Cleveland Browns, 38-14.

The 1970 season saw Roger once again on the bench for most of the year. Morton, starting all but 3 games along the way, paced the Cowboys through the play-offs and into Super Bowl V.

And then, as had happened the 4 previous seasons, the Cowboy bubble burst. In an error-filled game that neither team seemed to want to win, Baltimore finally outlasted Dallas, 16-13. The margin of victory had come on a field goal with 5 seconds remaining in the game.

As usual, Dallas fans were extremely vocal in their reaction to the defeat. Their frustration had now turned into open hostility.

The Cowboy organization was immediately swamped with letters demanding that Landry replace Morton with Staubach in 1971. But Landry simply shrugged his shoulders and set about preparing for the coming season.

Shortly before the 1971 campaign began, Staubach was growing quite restless. He figured it was now his turn to see what he could do.

"I believe very strongly," he said, "that I'm capable of winning with the Cowboys, of taking this team to a championship."

Roger was convinced he should be Number 1. Quite justifiably, Craig Morton disagreed. When asked about his rivalry with Staubach, Morton said, "He's going to have to do a lot more than he has. You know, he has to beat

me out. I don't have to beat *him* out."

During the exhibition season, Landry was constantly questioned by reporters eager to know who his starting quarterback would be. "I'm not going to rate Morton and Staubach for you," Landry said. "Maybe when the season starts, we'll go with both of them. If they weren't performing well, I might have a problem. I don't see any problem now."

During the 6-game exhibition season it looked as though Landry was right after all. The Cowboys won them all, with Morton and Staubach starting 3 times each. Their passing statistics were just about equal, too, with only a slight edge to Roger.

When regular season play was about to begin, Landry decided he would have 2 Number 1 quarterbacks. He would alternate them as he had done in the exhibition games.

One major drawback of the plan was the added pressure it would place on Morton and Staubach. Neither one would be able to play effectively if he realized that at any moment he might be taken out of the game. Neither would have the time to develop his rhythm and confidence.

Both Morton and Roger were unhappy with the idea. Morton stated flatly that he didn't like it at all. Roger said, "I'm not crazy about the 2 quarterback thing, but it's a step up from where I was."

As the pressure mounted, Landry found he had another problem to contend with. The entire team was upset. They needed to know who their leader was. Only then could they develop the timing essential to their intricate system.

The players seemed to have no preference. Either Morton or Staubach would be fine with them, but it had to be one or the other.

Don Meredith, now a sportscaster, remarked on television that he was amazed at the situation. He wondered why Landry hadn't been able to see which quarterback was better.

"It's Landry's responsibility," Meredith said, "to pick a quarterback. After he picks him, it's his responsibility to go with him."

Dallas opened the 1971 season with Morton at the helm, defeating the Buffalo Bills. Craig turned in a fine performance, completing over 70 per cent of his passes.

Now it was Roger's turn to start the second game against Philadelphia. On his very first pass play, Roger was knocked cold by an illegal forearm blow from one of the Eagle linemen.

Then Morton came in, completing 15 of 22 passes to lead Dallas to a lopsided victory.

In a post-game interview Roger said, "Getting hit like that hurt, but in a couple of hours I was okay. It's what it could mean in the long run. It might mean the end of me here."

The Cowboys came into the third game of the season favored to stop the Washington Redskins. For 3 quarters Morton failed to move the uninspired Cowboys. Roger got into the game in the fourth quarter and proceeded to lead the team to a touchdown. But it had come too late, and the Redskins gained a 20-16 upset win.

An unspectacular first-half performance by Staubach against the New York Giants gave Morton a chance to atone for his sloppy play the week before. Hitting Bob Hayes with a thrilling 48-yard scoring strike, Craig rallied the team to its third victory of the year.

The next game with New Orleans was one the Cowboys figured to win handily. But Morton failed to generate any attack at all, and Dallas left the field at half time trailing, 17-0. Although Staubach closed the gap a bit with 2 second-half touchdown passes, the Saints held on

to win, 24-14.

It was now clear that neither Morton nor Staubach was playing consistently under the 2-quarterback system. Still, Landry was reluctant to make a change.

The pressure subsided the following week as Staubach tossed 2 touchdown passes in a Cowboy slaughter of the New England Patriots.

For the up-coming Chicago game, Landry decided to use a quarterback shuttle system. Morton would take the first play of every series, Staubach the second, and they would alternate from there. And Landry would call every play from the sidelines.

Explaining his decision, the Dallas coach said, "We are going with the shuttle because of the many change-ups the Bears use on defense. This way we'll be able to combat that."

Before the game one of the Chicago players told a reporter, "I can't see how they can get any confidence in themselves by cutting it up that way." His opinion expressed perfectly what Dallas fans and players were thinking.

Although both quarterbacks played well under the circumstances, the experiment proved disastrous. The Cowboys went down to defeat for the third time.

In the fourth quarter Landry finally had abandoned

the shuttle, choosing Morton to rally the club. Craig tried valiantly, but once again the change had come too late.

With Dallas' record now at 4 and 3, it looked as though the team might not make the play-offs for the first time in 6 years.

The team was confused and demoralized. Forced at last to make the decision he had postponed for so long, Landry announced that "for the sake of continuity" he would use only 1 quarterback — Staubach.

Roger was elated. "It's fantastic," he said. "This is the first time I'm really the quarterback. If I make a few mistakes, I'll still be in there. I won't be walking a tightrope any more. This way I'll come through a winner."

Naturally Craig Morton was disappointed by Landry's decision, but he took it gracefully. "I'm behind Roger," he said, "and I'll do everything I can to help him."

Roger didn't let Landry down in the next game against St. Louis. He completed 20 of 31 passes for 199 yards, leading the resurgent Cowboys to victory.

The team continued to regain its momentum against the Philadelphia Eagles, adding another win to the record.

The next game with the division-leading Redskins was crucial for Dallas. The Cowboys had to win in order to keep their play-off hopes alive. And win they did by a score of 13-0. The following week Staubach once again led the Cowboy charge, this time over the powerful Los Angeles Rams.

The Cowboys were rolling now, and nothing could stop them. In their last 3 games of the season, they completely overpowered the opposition.

The regular season was over, and Dallas was riding a 7-game winning streak. Staubach had been sensational. He had proved that he was an exceptional leader, able to motivate the entire Cowboy squad.

His teammates responded to Roger's dedication to

excellence. Said tackle Ralph Neely, "Roger will sacrifice anything, even his own body, to win a game."

Roger had led the conference in passing statistics, completing a remarkable 60 percent for the year. During one stretch he had thrown 134 consecutive times without an interception.

But the real test for Roger Staubach was yet to come. Could he take Dallas all the way through the play-offs and the Super Bowl? Or would he, too, prove to be a loser?

As much as they admired Staubach, many Dallas fans did not think he could do it. Bitter experience over the last 5 years had made them accustomed to defeat.

Dallas opened the play-offs with a hard-fought 20-12 win over the Minnesota Vikings. Then they beat the San Francisco 49'ers, winning for the ninth straight time. It was Staubach who had made the difference in the 14-3 battle.

In one truly remarkable play, Roger showed just how proficient he is when the pressure's on. It was third down and 7 on the Dallas 23. Roger faded back to pass, but found his receivers covered. Circling as far back as the 3, he dodged one tackler, twisted past another, and then started upfield. In danger again, he reversed fields and darted for the sidelines, somehow managing to stay on his feet.

Then he doubled back again and tossed a perfect jump pass to running back Dan Reeves for a first down.

Anyone who had seen that exciting example of the "Staubach Shuffle" would never be able to forget it.

Now all that remained was the big game, Super Bowl VI. Before the game Roger seemed relaxed. "Personally, I kind of enjoy the pressure," he remarked. "I only hope I can react the way I should."

When asked how he thought he'd play, Roger said, "Every time I step on the field, I believe my team is going to walk off the winner, somehow, some way."

Over 80,000 fans were on hand in New Orleans that memorable afternoon in January, 1972, to see Dallas win it all. Everything worked perfectly for the Cowboys as they crushed an excellent Miami Dolphin team, 24-3.

Several Cowboys had been outstanding. Duane Thomas had run circles around the Dolphins. The entire Dallas "Doomsday" defense had easily stifled Miami's attack.

But the game's Most Valuable Player Award went to Roger Staubach, who once again had been the big difference. Accepting the award, Roger said, "That's the way it is in this business. When the team does well, the quarterback gets the credit. I'll take it, I'm not turning it down; but there are a lot of guys who ought to be in for a share."

For Roger, victory was sweet indeed. As he stood there on the field in New Orleans, he could hardly fight back the tears of joy that welled up in his eyes. It had been a long, lonely way back to the top.

When the whistle had blown, signaling the end of Super Bowl VI, all of the pain and frustration of the past had disappeared.

At last he had achieved his goal. He was now one of the great quarterbacks in football; and he would remain so for a long, long time.

JACK NICKLAUS
BILL RUSSELL
MARK SPITZ
VINCE LOMBARDI
BILLIE JEAN KING
ROBERTO CLEMENTE
JOE NAMATH
BOBBY HULL
HANK AARON
JERRY WEST
TOM SEAVER
JACKIE ROBINSON
MUHAMMAD ALI
O. J. SIMPSON
JOHNNY BENCH
WILT CHAMBERLAIN
ARNOLD PALMER
A. J. FOYT
JOHNNY UNITAS
GORDIE HOWE

superstars!
superstars!
superstars!

CREATIVE EDUCATION SPORTS SUPERSTARS

WALT FRAZIER
PHIL AND TONY ESPOSITO
BOB GRIESE
FRANK ROBINSON
PANCHO GONZALES
LEE TREVINO
KAREEM ABDUL JABBAR
JEAN CLAUDE KILLY
EVONNE GOOLAGONG
ARTHUR ASHE
SECRETARIAT
ROGER STAUBACH
FRAN TARKENTON
BOBBY ORR
LARRY CSONKA
BILL WALTON
ALAN PAGE
PEGGY FLEMING
OLGA KORBUT
DON SCHULA
MICKEY MANTLE
EVEL KNIEVEL